Our Earthly
Eyes

Our Earthly Eyes

A Compilation
Annie Hwang

Order this book online at www.trafford.com
or email orders@trafford.com

Most Trafford titles are also available at major online book retailers.

Author photo by Roxane Barth

Printed in the United States of America.

ISBN: 978-1-4269-4759-9 (sc)
ISBN: 978-1-4269-4761-2 (hc)
ISBN: 978-1-4269-4760-5 (e)

Library of Congress Control Number: 2010916668

Trafford rev. 12/15/2010

 www.trafford.com

North America & international
toll-free: 1 888 232 4444 (USA & Canada)
phone: 250 383 6864 ♦ fax: 812 355 4082

For Mom, Dad, and the Keller High Poets Society
For everything, for several things

I am
Down the road and up
the hill
I wait for you still
Wires 'round my fingers
Potentially lovely
Perpetually human
Suspended and open
Open

— Regina Spektor

Contents

Heaven

I Could Never Fathom Heaven

I could never fathom heaven,
while myself still treaded earth.
But I know my epoch of disbelief,
will, like my living, be reversed.

Is it faith that worry grows here?
that my doubts shall amount to no worth?
While my knowledge is still fed,
there shall be no mirth?

God expected of me, his child,
unseeing whole-hearted belief,
which I did, which I could,
besides the waver and it being brief.

But I have hope! And I know the truth,
that my incredulity,
will once it's being in heaven disappear,
and break my penalty.

A Little to Keep Inside

There is much we have to say
and little to keep inside,
as if we're all in a hurry
to leave parts of ourselves behind.

"God"

If he is the living truth,
then I'm the dying lie.
"Loving child," he croons,
and then goes ahead and makes me cry.

If he is anywhere inside of me,
then I must be turned inside out.
And if vast as the sea his love is,
then does he see that I've begun to drown?

(Incomplete. That's what this poem is: incomplete.
If you ask me, and I dare you to, why it is incomplete?
I say, grievances to this superior being is an endless streak.)

Retirement

When I retire from living,
I would return to my House.
Lay down all that I'd been given,
and rest all my limbs.

Time would be of Forever,
dreaming a certain course.
My grades always dependent,
on how free is my heart.

Perfect Mess

Today, I had a perfect mess of photo albums around me.
I was knee-deep into memories, and a couple jumped out.
There were black and whites, colors, and some
splashed with emotions.
I saw myself first in baby skin,
in silky dresses and satin ribbons,
in a white gown, then in wrinkles,
and I saw myself just yesterday.
There was one of my sister and me.
Fighting over a silly doll.
Its hair was long and golden, unkempt,
rough, partly curly, mostly colored.
Rainbow.
I giggled and snickered ridiculously over it.
No one else in the living room,
except myself and I.
I can laugh all I want.
I'm ninety-nine and the hell with everything,
the hell with the food.
the hell with the clothes.
the hell with the money.
the hell with stifling atrocious laughter.

I can feel it...
I saw some sort of blinding flash.
God took a picture of me right now,
sitting around pictures of pictures,
and he's saving it for me...
later, in heaven, lounging on some couch,
I'll sit around with photos of me like this,
and I'll stifle another laughter!
And another!
And another!
And I'll say: "That was fun.

That was life back then."
Hopefully then, I won't be so alone
as to let my silly self let loose.
But either way,
I'm sure I'll laugh at it.
Laugh at myself.
Because we all end up doing that.
Just doing that.
Just laughing at ourselves.. and that's that.
And that's all.

The Suspect

Out of the womb and into the crime scene,
they believe you are the suspect.
Evidence being that you were alive and breathing,
for your atrocious conduct, they must inspect.

Yesterday, were you alive?
Being alive means you must've sinned.
You can say the words you like,
but you do know, we have you pinned.

The day before that, you must've thought.
Things you thought we'd never find.
Your penalty is death, and death it is,
oh, you thought we were blind?

For your ancestors, dry your bones.
For the oxygen, work your limbs.
You feel you are more likely the victim,
either way, you would've sinned.

Pair of Feet

Dying at a pair of feet,
at the feet of God.

Bare, without a trace of labor,
bare, without a sock.

Are his fingers too?
His fingers soft as baby skin.

And his eyes, fairer than the moon,
glowing from within.

But all I see,
and so I wonder all,

because I see his feet,
and the rest just enthrall.

Is this how it feels to be dying?
First, you glimpse at his toes?

Then your curiosity lures you in,
to relieve of your repose.

And dying at a pair of feet,
struggling descends.

Fighting for what? For what, I know!
To the head, the eyes, I transcend.

Life and Death

I do not ask 'which is better',
for none satisfies to satisfaction.
If I was expecting half so pleasant,
then why does Death hold my attention?
The wonder was, and still is,
whether there's a difference or not,
between life and death, non-existent grace,
and everything else that can't be stopped.

Solution

Death is a box of matches,
to light in ecstasy.
That makes me none but an
eager, curious wick.

The wax is and never will be,
pain that buries me.
Memories that attempt to smother,
what life can't offer me.

Death melts away all that,
the fire asks nothing but my oxygen,
I give Death it, and Death gives me,
my final, bright solution.

Vineyard Sonata

I.

Venerable years really know
How to age a man.
In another world,
His reminiscence would glow:
They're bitter in every way, but still irrevocably sweet.
But in this town,
And like many towns,
A wine is sipped than remembered.

II.

Soft and guiding,
That northern star—
Bright and luminous,
Dark and inevitable,
Like this life so bizarre.

Genius

Genius was never recognized in its own time,
But it still haunts us today.
Dickinson, Poe, Clare, Sylvia Plath,
All who knew ephemeral death and eternal fame.

Remember

Remember, if at all you can
the voices which spoke to you at first
when your ears were alive.

Hope, if at all you must
when the musings you hold dear
are gone and society dried them all up.

Dream, if at all you should
because the world isn't satisfying enough
and this is the most you can think to do.

Cry, if at all you would
for the sake of a romanticist
in search of a true love, and you were a quiz.

Die, if at all you cannot
accomplish any of these tasks at all
and your heart cannot bear any more.

Live, if at all you cannot
even accomplish death because you refuse
to succumb to such flighty things.

The Sail and the Moon

I, the sail.
My God, the moon.
He shines upon a evening sea.
The more I swim a little forward
to reach that moon,
the farther away he seems to be.
Just a reflection, but I do not realize.
So close, I think all the time.
And when I near,
he disappears,
just a bleary image.

Personal Stalker

Death is so close to me
the distance is immeasurable.
He stalks my every move
and waits 'till time is favorable.

He does not especially despise me,
but also does not look with fond eyes.
With such a threat in each of my breath,
there is no telling *when* is my demise.

Simplifications

The artist is dreaming,
The musician is finding,
The poet is losing.
And God… he is watching.
Oh, he is always watching.

Promoting Death

Heaven is a broken clock
timeless and eternal.
A perpetual ray of sunlight
shines, splendid and graceful.
God is your holy guardian,
and there is everlasting youth.
Laboring is a forgotten idea,
and you are fed only the truth.
Your spirit is carefully gardened,
your legacy, lovingly seasoned.
The maternal angels caress you,
and every paradox is reasoned.

Holy Spirit

I do believe
there is a spirit in me
that speaks with a placate tone.
But a clamor (also in me)
disturbed this courier and pulverized
the creature to incomprehensible pieces.
Imagine syllables scattered
on a disheartened writer's page.
Then understand me for a second
that the spirit I called back,
could not be pieced again!

Church [Inspired by Emily Dickinson]

I heard the bell on the holy day
and questioned my presence here
in a four walled room, void of whom
they say can only be felt there.

Reality

Reality at its finest hour
Can brew the monstrous thoughts
Incoherent, but in one way, true:
That escape is the only way,
And escape, one must do

A Suicide Pleading Before a Jury in Heaven While in Hell

But world, but society, my dearest neighbor,
Think of me tenderly! My heart was mortal, and reality
Easily penned my tragedy!
Each day I lived, was a day I died— what a strange way to subsist.
Surely, you can forgive this once, the once in which I couldn't
persist.

The Blind Date

My relationship with God
is constantly a blind date -
- one day,
I ask him boldly and daringly
for his number and name -
- Yahweh,
but that is all he says
and his unwillingness makes me think -
- heartstrings
can't last long in a one-sided
relationship, though I do love him -
- in all my skin,
but why can't he love me?
Why must he be a secret -
- a weary mystery?

The Poet's Gift

When I leave, if in elegance,
or if in a simple cot,
there is nothing more I'll leave
than my wordy lot.

A singer leaves his music,
when the light is snuffed from his candle,
and though I am merely mortal,
a poet leaves her poems immortal.

Fragment

Imagine possessing a piece
but not the whole.
Curiosity would be the muse,
insecurity would be the fear.
And how incomplete the clause.
Thwarted, you wonder where the other is.
Despondent, you wonder if ever complete you'd be.

The Answers (haiku)

tell me the answers
where the road begins and ends
with your worldly eyes

God has No Color

God has no color,
but the palette of love.
His canvas is the face,
the many faces of us.
I am fair like
a dappled cloud -
and he, golden, like
a shade of the sun,
she, a dazzling
earthy brown.
God's skin is the skin of us.

Then It Should Begin

Then it should begin with
What started it
The seed and the egg
Sittings in one day
Led to the next
To stand before autumn
To think of yesterday.

Then Don't Ask

I don't pray anymore
It's not my task.
If it doesn't work one way,
Move onto the next.
If it won't be answered,
Then don't ask.

Somewhere

There is a point to life somewhere—
I saw it yesterday,
Lost it today,
Heard it call my name minutes ago.

The Meaning

I knew what it meant to live.
The thing that we had in common.
Like a flicker, it passed me,
in dutiful reminder.

The strangest sort--from Spring.
To the reflection of Winter,
everything that ceased to be--
caused a peaceful banter.

What I'd sought for.
Everything from the trees
to the floorboards of dead bodies.
A sheet of grime, unwanted.
Peeled itself, shed itself, gave into remedies.

I found peace within.
Within the unfolding, though it caused
a small commotion.
But we all can't leave
quietly, we must all leave behind
some sort of ruckus.

A brilliant light slapped
a brick inside my eyes.
Shattered--and ultimately,
opened face to the truth.

I was afraid of what I was leaving behind.
Oh...how I'd used to hate life.
You grow used to such things, I supposed.
But I accepted *meaning*, and shushed the strife.

A Stream of Consciousness

There's an equation running through my mind.
A stream of consciousness,
broken once in a while by a voice that notifies me of
chances, reason, and rhyme.
None of it that makes sense.
After all the struggles of trying to find myself,
or discovering identity,
making an imprint of your personality,
I have reached a conclusion that it is better left unknown.
If I don't like myself and that is all there is, then what will I do in
the end?
Some days, I have this strong need to purge myself.

Most of the time though,

I just want to sleep.
Tomorrow will be another day. (But I know a secret)
Tonight, when I sleep (There is a secret)
I will dream(a secret)
and tomorrow morning,
I will wake up.(Not unless I follow the secret)

Ode to the Star-catchers
[R.I.P. Emily Dickinson]

You think that
she was a mad woman.
Impartial to
reality and
buried in her own
burial of words
nonsensical
ramblings of
the intellectual
sort.

They're all
like that.

But I think
differently.

She knew
the ways of
star-catching.
And she joined
the stars
before
robbing them
of their light
as many poets
attempted to
do.

You see
I think she was
smarter
and wiser
than you
and me.

And instead of
kindly asking or
kindly begging
or kindly snatching
the stars of their
mysteries - she
joined them in
their midnight dances
and decided
she too
should be a star
in order to
shine like one.

And which
she now does
in her words
her works
and in our hearts.

Sometimes
you can see her
at night.
And you wish on her
without knowing
you are wishing

to join her
because you are
swamped
in the dread
of this earth.
While she glows
in her mysteries
and tales
she only whispers
to you
in dreams.

First I Will Be Autumn

First, I will be autumn.
I will shed my regrets.
Then I will be winter -
with death, comes birth.

I will sleep in the process -
and love in it too.
And come out of the cave
singing my song.

I Heard the Call

I heard a call
that emptied out
all of my soul.
And breathed into me
helium,
a new life
I had ahead.

I looked up

and touched the clouds
with the jungle of my hair
and I closed my eyes
but saw everything.

I shed

all of my skin and bone
watched as they limply hung
by the ligaments of nostalgia
but even that

I let go

to live again.

Earth

O God, My God

O God, my God, I say,
allow me to grieve in my human heart.
It knows no better than to do
what you told me not to do.

Desperate are the seasons,
that long to take their strides on earth.
While I, grieve and squirm around
for heaven to be my ground.

Element of Change

Hope is an element of change,
for change is the result of hope.
Prayer is one out of many,
if hope seems far, a way to cope.

In comparison to humans, hope is,
but a theory of manipulation.
If not used, it is only muse,
to be a facade of progression.

Hills are no barrier to change,
hills roll, you see.
But the stale water, stagnant,
has no fate, but to be deceased.

Are you in this too?
Are you an element of change?
The dragging darkness of eclipse
or the light of a new phase?

Shooting Star

Lovely things are always temporary.
Time, for them, is a shooting star.
Oh, how glorious are their ephemeral existences,
and how dreadfully do they depart.

Drowsy

Drowsy, drugged by reality.
All tentativeness beaten.
Heart succumbing morphine--that is
weariness from functioning.
Beat. Beat. Each heartbeat
that shrewdly blossomed inside of me,
now done with, now annihilated,
given away to languidness.
My poverty from illusions and dreams
drives me and sinks me to the floor
of reality. Sleep, they tell me.
Sleep. Eyelids that weigh a ton
descend to the pits where they
anchor themselves into dreamland.

Finished

I am finished with caring;
therefore, I am finished with losing.
The victory was wayward, but I have given it direction
by simply, losing way.
I foresaw the cycle doomed to its fate:
tossing from caring to losing to pain...
but now I am finished with caring.
Save yourself too, before it's too late.

Priorities

The list of my priorities used to be standing up.
But at some point or another,
the list tilted and became horizontal,
so that everything on my list spilt over
and came to be on the same plane, the same rank.
Now I am lost on whether which one to do first--
there is no first! All is the same,
all is ready, all must be done, all is priority.
Who flattened this list?! Who laid it on the ground,
so that the vertical order exists no more?
I realize... it was no one but I
who let the eyes off the child.
And in that split moment that I let go,
the flimsy list fell to the floor...
I should've kept the list in
a firm, stable mind--perhaps in card stock
or better, a cardboard area.
But the priorities dependent
on a weak, shaky surface,
were doomed to slip into hysteria.

Do Not Wake Me

Do not wake me,
I have not slept enough.
(to dream)
Do not touch me,
I have not loved enough.
(to hurt)

Pain has a Route

Pain has a route that twists
  once in anger
and once in sadness.

But the rest of the lonely road,
pain bends its knees in shame.

Brooding

Sad
Then Mad.
They breed
Numbness.
Why?
Then ask How?
They twist
into grievances.
There.
Where?
They point
to pandemonium.
Breathe.
Then Not.
The world teaches me
to succumb.

I Want to Be Free

I Want to be Free

I want to be free.
Free from the memories.

I want to grow.
Grow those glorious wings.

I want to fly.
Fly away from the past.

I want to forget.
Forget everything that binds me.

I want to be bound.
Bound to my forward dreams.

I want to dream.
Dream in nights that aren't a burden.

I want to sleep.
Sleep only because I want to.

Not because I need to.
But because I want to.

Earthly Eyes

She gazes upon heaven with earthly eyes,
and sees just as much the earth can see,
but translates the heaven through her heart,
and interprets the thoughts through her poetry!

Humans

It was midnight -
and I was surely asleep,
but my mind seemed to be
slightly awake
at that slight moment
of slight consciousness
that you later slightly
remember the slight
evidence
of there being
ghouls prowling
the carpet of
your New York apartment.
That night
when the apple from
the apple city
was about to be stolen.
That night
when the love from
the humanity
was about to be withdrawn.

The slightness -
as surreal it was
was also insoluble in
dreams for it was
indeed real -
monsters, they were.
They crept along the
sides of my gilt bed frame
and one of them suggested
slyly, "Let's take out
his heart!"

A yelp silently
surged and slipped
out of my throat -
but they were too focused.

Upon thoughts upon silence
the other one said
surreptitiously so that I
wanted to hear more:
"No! That is what
keeps him WEAK."

I would have denied
this and leapt at this
figure, intent on
destroying humanity -
but I couldn't
because my heart
indeed got in the way
and courage was besotted
and the empirical glass
shattered into fragments of
submissive fear.

The Painter and the Paintee

The painter looks to his subject
and says she looks scared.
She glances to her right and says
that, indeed, she is afraid.
But now that he mentions it
she is less troubled -
because he just confirmed her
humaneness and so she wishes
he would hurry on and paint her,
so she is caught in this warm
moment of embrace and understanding
between fellow, fearful humans
about how scary the world can be.

He picks up his paint brush
that has been dipped in a flourishing scarlet
and says that he knows how she feels
except he doesn't understand how in
all our mutual understandings,
we can't seem to pause and help each other
nor make a difference in the nightmare.

She nods, and he tells her to stay still.

A Battle in the Sky

The clouds fought a bloody battle
'twas no battle that's fluff and idle.
In fact, blood was spilt and stilled,
we saw it that evening, a setting thrill.

An Island

The sea surrounds me,
a salty mess.
My feet deep into the golden sand...
A balmy air of the breathing sky,
blue as the blue of sea of life.

The Rain

I miss the rain.
It really grows on you.
The constant pattering,
persistent whispering.
The rain never gives up.
The rain fell just for my little head,
It fell a long way from the
tip top of the sky,
the distance no one else would
fall for me.

Winter Breath

How can you feel so alone?
When this winter breath
encircles you?
They want to play
and distract your mind,
So you aren't cold anymore..

How considerate of them.
They twirl around,
They're just fine with the fact
that you breathe,
and the more you talk to them,
the more they exist.

The Womb of Seasons

Winter is the womb of seasons.
It bears the child of Spring.
Quietly, Winter nourishes it in toasty slumber,
finds a haven under snowy wings.

The Hardest Look

Even the hardest look wavers in the lake moonlight.
Darkness underneath my foot of the bridge,
calm and still and waiting patiently.
A white, unholy bird flaps its wings gracefully and glides across
the water,
the water forces its face to remain frozen.
But alas, a touch of the bird's dry feet awakens the lake.
This is the cue for me to talk.
But what can I say? The look is my answer for questions unasked,
the immobile exterior is my command to leave, and
the rounded knuckles, bearing veins on the surface are the details
to the conclusion of this meeting.
This is the cue for me to stay.
If I stay, those marble knuckles may come alive, flex,
and stretch to throw a punch to my flesh; the immobile body
may move again and move in exemplary agility towards
my frail, little bones and crash at full force into me; that look may
cut open a blood-thirsty stare that would bore into my soul,
closing and opening wounds, cutting up my scars,
if I stay. And those are the reasons I *do* stay
because they will make us both so so alive.

On the Verge

Sitting precariously in the grim two seconds,
upon lofty, horizontal stilts that line up next to each other,
flimsy, weak, bending..under pressures of a breaking heart.
Losing grip, slipping--two tears slide unto pale skin,
converging with the dry. A rumble of veins underneath.
This is--today--I saw my mother cry...

Summer Day

You think, maybe—
Miss Summer would like a sunny ride?
To the barbecue pit near Sandy's,
The smoke rings? The laughter and heat?
I wait in the coach for her, but it just rains,
Another spring day again.

Hummingbird

Whimsical and brilliant,
A hummingbird fleeting by
Busy with something we'll never know—
You blink and you miss a good-bye.

Autumn. Again.

Autumn in lipstick
kissed all my backyard trees.
Oh, the stains on their faces,
and some, in their blushes.

Grandfather

He's not my grandfather, but I wish my grandfather could garden.
My grandfather's dead.
The old man, wearing his wrinkled skin and wearing his hairless
head,
walks out once again
into the sunlight and crinkles his many-toed-crow-feet eyes
and coughs. It was originally a sneeze.
No sneezes for old people anymore.
The shriveling-nose costume may fall off.
He carries a water bottle full to the brim with water and
pours.
Pours.
Drip.
Second to last drop.
He spends the last of his youth
on this garden. Adolescence leaks out--
last drop.
I watch intently: my eyes focused entirely on the old man,
my almost grandfather. I, like other people, feel like he can be
watched
and he wouldn't notice. But I, like other people, fell for his clever
costume.
He turns around, feeling a youthful, curious gaze.
And I quickly look away.
The next day, I walk in his garden.

Alice

I tried to type 'alive'
but I missed the key.
As the title dictates,
I should write about Alice...
who is she?
The wonderland girl?
A blue cocktail dress,
well-polished black shoes
and a cupcake.
This isn't too hard.
What would I have done
if I had written 'alive'?
Sometimes, I like it
when things are laid out.
Thanks, Alive.
I missed the key again.
I hate my life.
At least this rhymes.

I'm Sorry

I'm sorry
and that is all.
If I knew why
I would say more,
but because I don't,
well,
I don't know anymore.

School Room

I try to make an austere heart
that knows duty before pleasure,
but it is fickle as a school boy
tied to a desk in the summer.

The Heart

the heart's syntax
is but a salty mess
the speechless speech of
? !/#
??
!
many questions
??? ? ??? ??
one answer
!
one answer that is a question
!(?)
the myriad of confusion
@ --?-!-!!-!--

Cross Pollination (haiku)

cross pollination
battleground of the beauties
pretty gets ugly

Love Ache

Missing something,
or someone,
dearly.

Don't know what
or who,
too surely.

Ode to Time I

Time, my enemy, my eternal foe, cannot stand still.
The cause of all my hopes that abrade to nil.

Desires on a String

There is a place out there for me.
It taunts my heart
with my desire
coyly on a string.

I'm not cat
but it makes my soul sing!

I Met a Steinway

There is nothing to
look ahead for
in the stark, blunt
buildings that surround
me, embrace me
with cold arms
as I walk in the
slabs of streets.

Then I observe
a Steinway in the
Square. I near it
curiously - I
meet a man sitting
on the leather chair,
poised. He is crying.
His long, slender fingers
slip across the keys,
barely touching,
barely missing,
and crying all the while.

Playing in a pool
of longing, yearning.
I wait for this melody
to pause, but it doesn't -
it is a pause in itself,
a breathing in the
sadness that engulfs
both of us.
I near him slowly
and discover he is

the man I hope to help,
and I stare into his eyes
and say, "And this
too shall pass..."

He looks to me and
says not a word,
his music grants me
stay, and I
get found in the
sound that wraps
around me -
steals the embrace
of this frigid city,
and tells me
that my loved one
is looking for me also.

Please

Please!
Please?
Please...

The ache
instilled in
this one word
throttles
the veins
of my poet's heart.

Ode to Walls

Walls swallow
walls breathe
walls witness
bound by the
unholy eyes
of truth.

We cover them with
frames, mirrors,
posters, paint
to avoid the past
to smother voices.

But they gaze
through the paint
and the frame
and the mirror.

And alone in a bare room
enclosed in the brick arms.

You face what you need to face.
You fall where you need to fall.
And become a piece, a part
of the walls.
Bound by the
unholy eyes
of truth.

The Lone Art

You aren't lonely,
you are free.
The night is a gate,
open's the sea.

And while some may weep,
and be chained inside.
You sit lofty
in your spacey mind.

Sleep--death--a lone sport.
Some Pitifuls find it a way to cope.
Dream--life--a majesty,
they're my kind of company.

You aren't lonely,
you are free!
like the moon at night
bright, at ease.

While some may see
the moon caged in the dark,
it glows freely,
solitude is an art!

Word

Words could be my greatest weapon
as are knives with a surgeon.
And beautiful, the poetry.
as beautiful, the pained debris.

The Worst

I know I said the worst there ever is
to say.
Everything from your flaws to everything you wanted
to fix.
And I had understanding meanwhile.
You know I did; I know I did,
but I don't know what I was doing at the moment.
My mouth was oily,
my heart was compact,
I had no idea and I lost myself.
I'll tell you something scary...
I don't know who I lost myself to!
If you know, let me know.
But if you want to forget this,
please do.

A Proposal

I proposed to lose myself
In the forest over there,
Teeming with playful shadows,
A lone piper's lair.

I was invited after the first broken heart,
Called over by another Despondency,
The sought welcome wasn't what greeted me,
But what held onto me.

Poetry Differs

I try to fit as much meaning I can
to each word and phrase,
but to every audience, poetry differs,
as do the speed of different days.

Water and Poetry

I drink water when I write poetry.
Kind of strange, seeing as I'm not talking.
But once in a while,
my brain screams "dehydration!"
And my fingers anxiously grip the glass
and rush the water down my throat.
Stomach gurgles.
Poem remains the same in mid sentence.
This is just
-drinks water-
an observation.

Self-Assault

Nights of sitting alone in the dark,
I've framed myself to be of fault.
Because thoughts lead to one another,
With no one else to blame in self-assault.

Daylights aren't welcome to the wronged,
Just a cleavage to escape.
But when the night returns after sunset,
Liability revisits to take shape.

Backyard

Thorns guard that deserted place,
Owls hoot to that grave,
And the moon can hide behind that grass so tall,
I can't see clearly to the other side,
So dense— like my mind— so dense
Full of weed.

To Disappear

On days like these,
I sit on the edge of my bed
and feel like it's the edge of the world.
I lean a little forward,
and the whole world creaks,
and I lean a little back,
and the whole world is dented.

Do you want me in
or do you want me out?

What is Night?

I wouldn't know.

A sanctuary of layers under comfortable memories
to many, but to me, a mysterious sanctity and like
a god's place: holy yet unholy, known yet unknown?

Suspended in the frozen air, no brisk paces for me,
dazed and in the twilight zone, this is what it means to be alone--
the night is agape with my soul too, none of us possess water.

Kindle my heart, will you? Help me dream pleasant things.
I am lost and threaded in a maze of imaginative fringes
and am a foil for the specks of reality.

Call me forward, will you? I cannot find myself.
Given direction, perhaps I'll head-- one place or another,
help. The sky is gruesome, a vast abyss. Help.

What is night? My daily demise in a dark room,
to be unearthed in the morning and buried in a tomb,
soon. I will return again to my only company

the night. Oh lovely night. My irony, my ache,
reveal yourself too me, but not too much at once.
I will tilt my head, walk into me with all the pleasant dreams...

Poetry Used to Be

Poetry used to be
like singing a song for me.
Each syllable carried a certain note
and I could hum the verses
right off the pages!
But now
poetry seems to me
like a rejected wad of gum,
spit onto the lines like trash
because rhymes lost their drum.

Explaining

How to explain my feeling as of now...
that it is almost like noxious waste
hurled into a vacuum that was not immunized
to anything. That the order and direction of my thoughts,
synthesized and intellectual, were suddenly
thrown into a schism of befuddled theories.
"And I'm tired of dying; let me die, so I can live!"
cries my stocked up shelf of miseries.
This is how I feel: that I cannot explain.
Almost everything is surreal, except the very pain.

My Overture

The stainless sea
The infallible sea
cannot move aside for me.

This emergency
My overture
into Fate afflicted society.

Cries!
every
tir
ing
circle of
unappreciated
irony.

Metallic
skin -

not
me.

I am only
a child

released

(pet
fish)

into

The stainless sea...
The infallible sea.

Becoming a woman...

My Goddess
keeper of my wishes,
the torch of my heart,
the Sappho to my poet's soul,
teach me.
Teach me to be like the Sahara--
beautiful and vast with golden, jeweled skin,
and teach me too--
how to be unforgiving and challenging.
Teach me how to control the depth of my oasis--
when to store and when to give,
teach me,
to be a master of my senses.

To Fellow Poets

Because you are a poet,
I want to give to you, In my mutual poverty,
a million dollars worth of understanding.

If the money were real, you could be
kept away from your locked-up secretary
work, and you could be instead at a vast paper

writing away your mind,
and weaving away your ideas and gathering
the fibers of your poetic nature.

I know this, so I give you,
symbolically, all these jewels and gold
to free you from your onus of living up to standards

and to release you like a sacred monarch
onto hedonistic hills and intrinsic islands,
so you may be a poet there, my fellow connoisseur.

A Broken Compass

Where do I go?

Armed with my peach skin.

Just as bruisable,
just as moldable.

Where do I belong?

No one to call me from there.

Wherever *there* may be,
whoever *they* may be.

The Days When Poetry Drags

The pot is stirring rather slowly today,
dragging the ingredients through.
Pulling, pushing, opposite factors
that hinder the cauldron's brew.
And though the body is ready,
and the hand ripe as berries,
no poetry today, no sir.
The pot is simply not ready,
it is still coalescing,
and the mind is still unsure.

January 20, 2009.

The Inauguration of President Barack Obama.

It's flesh to flesh
but there's also so much more to it.
Men, women, and children huddle in gloves and scarves--
breaths twirl visibly in the icy air.
The atmosphere of the event harnesses joy, common ground spirits.
Some proof of this may be
involuntary tears,
closed eyes in hope
and folded hands of open-eyed prayer.
And before their awe, a man is standing in specks of
red, white, and blue.
Every word he speaks is a mere echo
of every other man, woman, and child in the room.
It's heart to heart,
it's mind to mind,
and there's nothing less to it.

The Decision

I loved, because I could.
Then shortly after,
I cried because I would
not laugh - and that is all.

Pain is Beautiful Like

Pain is beautiful like
the way the injured sun
in all its bleeding glory sinks down,
but this is spectacular to our eyes.

And the way Atlas holds up the Earth,
his muscles spasmodically jumping,
and his body rotting away, but
it must be the perspiring look on his face
or whatever it is, the earth is
so marvelous in all its bearings.

We observe the lamplight
and awe at its occasional flicker and
muse to ourselves that indeed,
the burning of many moths is sparkling
and majestic - pain is beautiful.

Apologizing

Apologizing is like
holding your breath
then exhaling -
then questioning
the flow of your blood.

Spring's Coming

Wading through the pool
of Spring.
Brushing up against
the lovely things.

Breaking the crest of
the pond's surface,
my fingers trail
a line of bliss -

the woman in me
brought forth
and the child in me,
readily yours -

My heart is speckled
chartreuse,
flourishing with my soul,
infused.

Dying for the Mystery

When I asked you why
the sea was so wide and deep
and full of mysterious things
you did not answer.
When I asked you why
we tried so hard to be
wide and deep and full of mystery
you said we were jealous of the sea -
and that made sense, really.
I am indeed jealous of the sea
and its essence, a voyage in itself.
It does not depend on anything
or anyone - and it needn't ask for help.
I am indeed jealous of the sea
and the adventure it holds selfishly.
And the rest of us who travel upon
the waves - are willing to die for the mystery.

Missing Child

The worst feeling is to know
that somewhere out there
the one you love
is still alive,
perhaps almost
dead
or still dead -
but nonetheless -
it's about the chance.
And so you cannot take a step
for any other reason
or in any other direction
but that direction that
serves to find the child -
missing. Dying. Living?
And tonight, again,
you are in the cab -
driving. Looking.

Perhaps the Poet Writes

Perhaps the moon shines
Not because it wants to shine
But obligation in all its dreariness
Forced it to.

Perhaps the sun rises
Not because it wants to rise
But because slumbering below horizon,
It wasn't allowed to.

Perhaps the bird flies
Not because it wants to fly
But because there is a secret he must
Flee from and to.

Perhaps the poet writes
Not because she wants to write
But the streams of imagination forgets
She has reality, too.

Gray (senryu)

She only blew half the candles,
As if to save the other half of her head
From being covered in gray.

Curtains

They only show a sliver of a picture through the window, but
They do what Life couldn't— cover the other half I don't want to
know.

Mountains

The mountains are honest,
I notice, as I climb higher.
The steeper it gets, the harder it is,
only a life story can compare with this.
Wind snatching, cold biting,
the near-end and all has wilted.
Mountains don't conceal,
the end is difficult--'tis what they reveal.
But if you rest at the peak,
and swipe your eyes across the land below,
it's beautiful, breathtaking! Mountains show...
this is how everything in life goes.

War Days

Through the window, young,
everyone's had a say in this war.
If they quieted, then they stood
for what the war was for.

It's summer and we stole it from ourselves,
there is wooden laughter.

Through the door, old,
we blackened the patch of grass.
It's over and all, but,
no one's truly, long glad.

It was a fire, we poured oil ourselves,
to wonder what it was after.

Poet's Block

I haven't touched a poem,
for a poem never touched me.
I couldn't give it respiration,
for none gave me inspiration.
My heart longed to compose a poem,
a poem longed to bear my tone,
but neither moved,
stalemate ensued,
I haven't touched a poem.

The Beach Sunset

I witness the reunion of the sun
and the sea. I stop in my run
and sit. Tangent on the glassy surface
the sun kisses the crests. Shy sea turns a shade of red, pearless.

I Knew Beauty

I knew beauty once I felt it
Because beauty itself took long to seep through
For connection with the eyes is fast and swift,
But the touch with the heart is slow and true.

Thrice

You asked me about the time thrice now,

Do you Know of Love

Do you know of love?
I wouldn't know— it's only my first life—
Oh, my only life.
Do you know of life?
You wouldn't know— you're still here—
You're not dead yet…fine.

All We Want to Do

Sleep is all we want to do
when the rest is against us.
Let our faith say 'no' and our hope say 'yes'
and ask, where is love?

We want to fall in to
the deepest slumber possible.
And wake up, forgetting ourselves
wake up farthest away from tomorrow.

We don't want any dreams
but the darkest blackness there ever is
and if they show us a better world,
we say, we don't want any of this!

We know better; we know there's a flaw...
sleep is the second best before death.
But death is a sin, sleep is revival,
we lay down our head.

And close our eyes...our earthly eyes.
And don't open them for the skies.

Buzzing Bee

Wading out to the sea.
Death is that summer bee.
Droning in a sweet sound,
sweet as the honey off this ground.

I stare ahead and eyes meet sun.
sinking, sitting near the ground.
My time here has gone,
and now tranquility will come around.

Tree Barks

Rough,
calloused,
what have
they
done?

Liberty to Cry

I ask for the liberty to cry.
Without having to worry about
the bleary redness of my eyes
or the expectations of having to
explain exactly why...
Please, I ask for the liberty to cry.
That is, I ask for the option to
be absent at Tomorrow.
My excuse is that I'll be busy
attempting to relinquish my sorrow.

1:00 A.M.

Suddenly
at 1 in the morning
a yearning inside of me
awakens - and
tears create the trails
of their exodus down my
high cheek bones and to
the waterfall off the crest of
my lips, and I
wish for so many things
and at the same time, I
cry at the beauty of this longing
that cannot be answered
when it is not in question form
but simply, in a statement
that is not a statement -
more in resemblance of
a sigh.
I, am now rolling over
this time, with the weight
of the tears on the side
of my face - and I
can feel the crackling
of the wet meeting the dry.
Of this yearning
that is a sigh.

When it Kills You Slowly

Change has come
and before we know it
more of it happens.

I sit by the fire
knowing but not knowing
feeling old but just the same.

Contradiction is life.
But life is not contradiction -
what did I tell you.

Live your life -
it tells you encouragingly -
when it kills you slowly.

Afraid of the Sea

I saw a boat on a hill
and thought of you.
Remember when
we used to sail
on land? We were
both afraid of the sea.

At night, I see a star
in the dark mast
of Earth's sail.
You and I
we are in the same
boat. Don't be
afraid, Love.

On War

Now it's not pain.
Now it's numbness.

Now it's not war.
Now it's treading.

Now it's not sharpened blades.
Now it's the unloaded gun.

Now it's not sadness.
Now it's the unspoken.

Now it's not about you.
Now it's not about me.

Now it's about everything around us -
and how we've stained it.

That Feeling

That feeling - where you know you're next.
        when you suddenly shut up.
        when you consider the consequences.

Us

I Was Made

I was made only half done.
The other half of me
lives inside a love of mine
soon to fulfill my half-ish needs.

She has what I do not
and it is no competition
which heart beats the loudest
in the love of our completion.

You Are

Friend, you're a secret to me!
As I may be to you.
And our distance, though from toe to toe,
never serves me to see you through.

Spoiled

The sun spoiled the sky,
like you have I.
No blue in me anymore.

I thank and I kiss
good-bye dark abyss,
I have a love at my door.

Come in and dream
as I have dreamed
the dreams that keep you asleep.

Dispel those creatures
those nightly monsters
that chill me, kill me, deep.

And love me,
a bucket full
no ribbon at a time.

So that at once,
I may be bright again,
the touch of sun to the sky.

A Man to a Woman

There is a heart in you that I looked for
a heart in you that sings.
It's warm and ringing, wild and free,
controlling uncontrollable things!

In Love

I don't really mind that I'm not in love..
or that I possess any, or that someone possesses me.
In the end, we both know, but only I can see,
that I'll be losing little, and you'll be losing everything.

When Men Don't Love

Flowers lose themselves
when they don't bloom.
And dying, they pride in themselves
what others see as gloom.

Horses are not horses
unless they are ridden.
And still in the barn, they sit,
as if life were a given.

Men cease to grow and learn,
the moment love is forgotten.
And rotting before soil is met,
men miss an early heaven.

How Human You Are

It is beautiful, your flaw.
How human you are!
There is a look in you of guilt
and laughter in your bones,
you are alive.

And when angry, you show.
Crinkles of smiles, apropos.
Lovely, your bashfulness.
You are free, no vows in you,
human as can be.

The Rumors of Love

I have not been scorched by the passion of love,
nor have I been carried afloat by its celestial lightness,
but I have heard such rumors.
They say the body's eyes become paralyzed,
and the hazel stones bore into only one other pair.
Love, they say, becomes a noun, adjective, name, verb.
Love becomes a place in which two souls swarm.
Love, by the sounds of it, or the fond gaze in which these rumors
are told,
seems to be existent in this world. Seems to be the most beautiful
thing--
enchanting, a heart-succumbing morphine. Love..
shall I go find you, or will you come find me?

I Loved Love

I loved love in relentless passion.
If love *was* passion, then this was it twice.

I believed in immortality and colors,
Not the sulphur of skin, the cardinal of blood.
Everything but.
Ideas and terms and thoughts had colors too.
They brushed across the canvas of my heart:
What more could I want?

I ended up wanting flesh.
Like others, I sought to feel the shell of bodies:
They called it skin, said it was a river of its own.
I realized love was truly immortal,
But the heart of man could live just as long.
Whilst the man could become both flesh and bones and idea,
Love could not.

But worse than abandoning…
If the heart of man should fail mine,
Then I know the ancient runes.

What is not real may be easier to believe,
For we all have the fairies perched in us,
And that the flesh and bones may rot and wilt,
But the thought of it all…may last forever.

Love, how loyal, as long as the mind is,
love stays there, that if my heart should ache,
Comforts me in elegance and fashion,
Old tradition, old folklore.

Old Friend

You are not the same to me anymore.
Of course, I took Change into consideration
when I promised you'd be like my sister,
when I promised I'd love you like my sister.

I thought, if anyone could overcome the misery of distance,
I could. I am immune to it by now--
everyone is gone from me. If anyone could love
unconditionally, eternally from far away,
I could. But that was before things changed.

I know now that the flower can only be appreciated fully
through sight or smell, through the touch
of silky petals. I know that the Spring's veil
of beady rain can only be felt by
the person who is there in full, peach flesh.

I know now that no power of understanding
no matter how immense or great in profundity
can overcome the human's weakness of the five senses.
I can say I *understand,* but if I really do or not,
if I really did or not, has become a loss,
will become lost by the decision made today.

Friend, you are a distant memory. I should
learn to let you go, learn to stop wanting more.
And there is no reason why I deserve your guilt.
So if we could just cleanly end it here...
so I don't make wasteful time over and over again,
sifting the same old, tiring dustpan.

I Am Afraid to Breathe

It's not that I'm not breathing,
it's just that you're too dream-like.
I feel if I breathe out,
you'll blow away from my sight.
And if I blink to bring life back to my eyes,
I'm afraid you'll disappear.
Is there a safer way to ensure,
that you are mine, my dear.

Brilliant Eye

If you pass by someone
with a brilliant eye,
that gleams at the recognition
of your very own eye,
then don't you think
it'll be swell to stop
and say 'hi'?

Winter is a Promise

Winter is a promise for spring
so may my departure be of assurance.
And allow us to depart with hazel eyes
the ones I met you in.
Don't cry, love. Instead, bid good-bye with a solemn kiss,
departures don't ask for a surer bliss.

When Saying 'No' to Love

When saying 'no' to love,
one must consider,
the most drastic effects.
A bruised friendship, and many a laughter,
whisked away to forget.

And upon announcing so,
one must harbor,
the best causes for such reason,
a pained relationship, and now a loss to come,
is it duty or is it treason?

And when thinking over all,
your reply starts to waver,
you must now consult your heart.
Nostalgic slides slip slyly by,
to have said 'yes', but to love 'no', and why?
He awaits your response,
the most ardent pursuer,
as he peers into your soul.
And it is upon that feeling, if his gaze is piercing,
and not warmth that you feel, say 'no'.

Distant Relationship

Love over a thousand miles
is like butter spread thin.
The more bread there is to cover; fear!
The more likely love may disappear.

Overdue

My heart did not break.
A mold grew in my heart.
The wait, the anticipation, the yearning—
Too dense to break into shards.

Tall Love

I
Fell
For
You,
My
Sweetest
Fall.
My
Love
For
You
Is so
Tall.

To a Friend

But you have a life too...
I apologize, sometimes, I forget.

And those days when I forget,
I get lost in wonder and my eyes dim.
My mind wades around in a dirty pool of
thinking, wondering, mostly worrying,
"What did I do wrong?! How stupid of me..
I'm so uninteresting, I don't deserve her..."

But you have a life too.
I apologize, sometimes, I forget.

Only Fame

There is only one person that knows me.
The knowledge is deeper and more profound
than those of notorious celebrities.
There is only one person that says to me
"I love you and you will be mine forever."
And I am the only fan who can say the same to her.
I am known by one and loved by one,
but my only fame satisfies me just the same
as the celebrities' with their surplus fame.

The Prediction

How is that I am able to miss you
as I stare at your timely face? You are here,
and I am here too...what is so hard to embrace?
My heard is shrouded with a dull ache
that squeezes out each shrewd beat,
almost suffocating, I worry: there won't be a you and me!

Missing in Action (M.I.A.)

Particularly today, I longed to fall in love.
But I could not fall in love without committing a sin.
The sun was merry with the clouds,
the grass whispered secrets to his lover, the rose.
Is there no love for me? Even concrete buildings
hug slim alleys. The flower pot is visited by the wind,
and to the waves, fish wave their fin.
I have no lover to gaze fondly on, though my eyes are ready!
I have no lover to douse with gifts, none to trust always steady,
and while every lover sings of their pleasant other,
I simply wait to be discovered.

Frail Women

The men, the lot
fall for the frail women.
Women who can't take care of themselves.
Women who dream but little dreams
that fly within the caged cell.

How about me?
Me, for a woman.
Once tamed, I can be as frail as her.
Though she may flee the moment set free,
once loved and loving, I stay forever.

Can I Simply Say?

Can I simply say "I love you"?
without further ado.
Without making a fool out of myself
as I already feel I do.

And can I just say
that "I have no explanation.
This love is rather unclear,
it's rather too random."

But it's there! Nonetheless..
like how we all try to search for ourselves.
We are all here, aren't we?
It's just that we need more time,
we just need some help...

For So Long
for Jackie Johnson

When you've missed a friend for so long,
it feels strange when you meet them.
Feels strange like you lost a hobby,
a part time job, a pastime...
you come at a loss of words,
loss of eyes, and loss of motion.
You never thought to say to them
things that you *actually* thought,
though you'd saved it all up for this moment.
Your eyes don't know where to place their gazes,
for it was always placed on pictures
or crumpled up letters--never on faces!
Your hands, foolish in their behavior,
don't know where to go. Always,
they had been on gift wrappers
or white envelopes, or tangent to
blotchy ink of pen pal letters...
Friend, by us being together,
you really do pull me happily apart!

Lie

I hoped it was a lie.
Couldn't you see it in my nervous eyes?
A light
flickered!
Popped!
And knowing it was the truth,
the fingers that had been choking each other
under the table--the battle ground of expectations--
paused. They released the breath each had been taking from each
other:
the one side of me that was telling me to let go,
the other side of me that was telling me to just believe.
Guess who won? Guess who you let win?

Subway

She was
in a sun dress with a daisy hair accessory
dangling off of her ginger curls;
an Audrey Hepburn glow.
Her pale legs crossed at an intersection of
dainty ankles, wrapped in glossy straps of summer shoes.
The pinkish hue of her enthralling skin
was unfortunately covered by a sheer, pristine blue cardigan.
Her sun hat completed her sun dress or the other way around
like how her eyes completed her lips or the other way around.
Glassy eyes of priceless emerald gems shone brightly.
She did not smile.
I was about to dive pleasantly into the sea of her existence,
to observe the petals of her flower, but suddenly.
A subway paused in between us. I felt like a porcelain figure
dropped to the floor.
As the subway sped again,
I waited to be picked up and smoothed--polished.
But she was gone.
Into one of those windows, into one of those lives.
I worried for her safety, I worried for her for many things...

Absence

On the days you are not here,
you must be over there,
doing important business.
I know, because I do
moon-talk, star-talk,
they tell me things.

But the sun, isn't on my side.
Each morning, she says
"another day gone!"
Another day gone without you
and another day to face
in your absence,
without the warmth of your embrace.

But it helps, you know,
having forgotten the warmth.
It helps that now each day
is each month and each month
is a year. It helps.

Especially if you have a large calendar
like mine.
Just a couple of more pages,
just a couple of more suns,
and you'll be home, right?
You'll be home...

Even the Roses

even the roses, so proud in their beauty
fold inwards like careful origami
and stay shushed

the train that passes by today
greets all the shadows in mourning
and slow down

the earth in its daily routine
stop the shifting of soil and pause
and grieve awhile

but you
you couldn't stop for me
could you

you forgot

you forgot and it's my turn
to say that's okay
people forget

but you shouldn't have but
you're not like the roses
that i thought you were

eternally beautiful and humble
or like the train
you don't have a gear in you
that slows down
or like the dirt you don't
have a place to be stepped on
i must be all that for you
what you couldn't be

We Are Close

We are close to our ending,
but both of us,
afraid to be the first,
wait for each other.

It's like the second when
someone, a kind someone
waits for you to pass through a door held open
but you're a kind someone too...

and there is a split second of
telepathic communication
"alright, I'll go first"

but we're not telepathic,
close friends aren't.
Only strangers.
Close friends,
the closer, are closer
to misunderstanding.

I don't know whether I should go first
in this balloon, inevitable in its deflation
One thing's for sure
we're both tired of dragging this around
our ankles, our hearts like we're bound
by responsibility (we never had any)
by duty (what is duty)

She Caught Stars

She caught stars
in her soft, pale hands.

But the only things I could catch
were earthly.
(fireflies)
(soil-bound leaves).

I dreamed of nearing her
in all my sainthood.
(If I had any)

I dreamed of touching her
in all my purity.
(If I was any)

Our spirits so far apart
yet my yearning so dear.

I wish to catch stars.
So with her soul, I can adhere.

My Ache, My Irony

My ache,
my Irony,
reveal yourself to me.

I'm curious to know
and I'm curious to find
who you are hiding inside.

Living inside you is a soul
I know
I don't know

My ache,
my irony,
reveal yourself to me.

Allow me to foil
your dispatched pain.
Let me be your reverie.

My night,
and my only,
I herald remedial dreams,

will you let me in?

Secret

This can be our little secret
you and me.
Our existence
lovely.

This could be what we smile at
while others wonder.
With frowns on their faces
torn asunder.

This could be that moment
in a picture.
I could be your ultimate seize
and you be my final capture.

This can be our little race
both of us winners
you and me
lovers.

Your Nomadic Heart

Your nomadic heart

makes me cry.

Tears of shame
    loneliness
    stormy
    violence
    fury
    hopelessness.

My sound-proof heart
who will hear these cries?

Your habit,
and now, my demise.

Suicide

My suicide--
letting you leave.
Listening to the suitcase
clasp. Suffocating
under the stuffed memories.
The aching soul--
and the suffering heart,
why...do I pull
myself apart?

In a Certain Angle of Light

In a certain angle of light,
I am see-through.

You were that light,
and you saw me through.

The forest teeming with
the brightest sort of light

my soul glazed with your stare
and my eyes blinded by your heart

This is how it feels to be loved
to be profoundly understood

This is how it feels to be understood
to be luminously loved.

Love's Dialogue

Are we in heaven?

No.

Are we near it?

Maybe.

Are we nearing it?

All the time.

Are we in love?

Yes

Last Night

Last night,
I sailed on your skin

the sea of blushing peaches.

Today,
I anchor myself next to you,

the shore of unfailing promises.

Let You Go

I don't think I'll be able to live

knowing I let you go.

I don't think I could've lived

in anxiety, you might go.

I Held the Sun

I Held the Sun

I held the sun
between my fingers.

Smaller than I expected
and cooler too.

Bringer of our light,
courier of days

rays that herald the future
settings that paint the twilight

But compared to me -
my love

how small it was.
Like a pebble.

But compared to you -
your eyes

how dull it was
like a stone.

You and I
we make something greater

greater than the sun.
greater than the twilight

and the dawn that wakes us...
we awaken love.

Sparkling Cider

Sparkling cider is your bonny face,
crisp and fresh with a tangy flavor.
I lean over to take a sip, from your
glass bowl with divine lips -
 and taste instead, sweet apple tarts -
a whole new dish of your refreshing heart!

Hypothetically

I kissed you.
Molten amber stared back at me,
quizzically.
"What the hell
did you just do?"
I...I was
kissing you?
There is a loud smack
and sparks on my face.
You walk away
telling me to mind my place.
Thank God -
it's hypothetical.

Silly Love Talk

"dear love"
i say
and some other
little words
that follow
such a passionate
tone.

"yes, love?"
she says
ignoring my
little words
that scattered
such a paramount
matter.

"i forget"
i state
honestly. because
it is hard for me
to remember
when seeing in her eyes -
ember.

"oh"
says she
to my silly remarks
but does not think this
a waste of time
instead goes about being -
divine.

I Loved You

I loved you
until you
told me you didn't
love me.

Now I move on
so easily.

Was this love
just an auction?

StayClose

Thespaces,theybotherme
stayclosemydearies,don't,foramomentthink,
I'lleverletyougo,andyoumuststay.
Eachspaceisarisk,yousee
Youmightgrowwingsandfleefromme
You'reallIhave--you'reallI'lleverneed
juststayclose...stayclose,mydears.

Friend (senryu)

Poetry, aren't you my friend?
Talk back to me!
I am so lonely...

A Pail

Do I need you?
That is,
do I need a pail
with a hole on the bottom,
unable to store water -
or life - or my love?

Tulips (haiku)

I did kiss tulips.
One red and the other pink.
Both did love me sweet.

End of the Tunnel

I'll meet you at the end of the tunnel
I hope I take the right route.

If I don't,
think of the days I loved you.

If that hurts,
think of the life before me and you.

Smile for Me

Smile for me
once more.

I miss its
splendor.

Simple it had been
simple it is now

but ample in its twitch
and profound in its vows.

But I Do

How can I miss you when we've never met?

How can I call your name when I don't know it?

How can I think of you when I don't know who you are?

How can I pray for you when I don't know your situation?

How can I want to be friends with you when I don't know you?

How can I wish you liked me as a friend when you don't know me?

How can I still think of you and your words -

when you don't mean to say them to me or anyone else?

I Cannot Love You

I cannot love you as you love me
For my love is none but a wanderer's song
Those songs with endless choruses,
That sing of the same memories over again.
You'd get tired of me soon, I'm like that month that brings you ice
You'd only find me prickly, and want to get rid of me.
And we'd be both disappointed, me, in my own fall.
Yours, that were in expectations that were replied by
My wanderer's songs, with the same old chorus.

Kind You Are

Kind you are until the end
The very end where you say good-bye,
That you do not re-enact a charming kiss,
But rather you turn a promising eye.

To My Journal

Silent companion,
Acknowledged one,
My hand betrays and withdraws.
Symptoms of such,
I loved you much,
But not enough to write all.

This Obsession

All my friends could not understand
My dire longing to hold your hand.
And if a kiss was to be far away
My friends would have my soul to tame.
Every mistake you committed
My friends revealed them to me and admitted
They were scared this love would do me harm
For I am chasing you, who is flawed.
Couldn't they see though that my obsession
Was for your love and imperfection?

Peer Inside

They say a person's kind heart,
Their inside is all that matters.
Doesn't matter if they're blue skinned,
Belly pierced, a leg shy, or fatter.
Well, you see there's this kid named George
Who thinks we'll make a great pair
But I have a hard time peering into his heart
And to see beyond his mole and hair.

Overdue

My heart did not break,
A mold grew in my heart.
The wait, the anticipation, the yearning—
Too dense to break into shards.

Breakfast and Reconciliation

There was more to the breakfast than just
toast, eggs, and orange juice.
A silent confrontation, muted confessions,
it was all to bring last night to a truce.

Carousel

for Mary Hannah McWilliams

It's, in many terms, difficult to explain.
For endless days in some barren desert,
I was spinning, round and round. Dizzy,
and ultimately, sick with my own thoughts.
They were renewed with the same old songs,
the same old horses, and the people. It was almost
a rerun of a collection of yesterdays.
And as it should, by nature, or by condemnation,
this carousel of my heart began to rust.

Pain is like that. You live and you live and
live some more, and the next thing you know,
there's a knife to your throat. And the hand
is your own. Raspy breaths, wading through mud.

And then.

The one I thought I knew the least,
began to know me best. Because I let Him know!
I told Him how much I needed.
How much I couldn't live without.
And then the carousel. It paused.
Someone was ready to hop on.

When I say, "Who are you?"
I don't mean it in a way of name or age,
but I mean: what is that smile you harbor?
Do you know me? Because I feel like I know you
I feel like I've asked for you all my life.
To the rust, you are " the oil that maketh
his face to shine." (*Psalm 104:15*)

I love you. I can spin round and round and
round any day. I am moving, but not moving forward.
That seems about right. I want to amble in this moment
all my life. It's difficult to explain
or express, but it's not impossible. Because
you're not impossible, and, and, and...
you're all that the human asks of his creator.
And all that the creator needs to give.

This is Romance

This is romance: the kitchen floor.
The running mascara on fat lips.
I scare myself in the wet, pooled tiles.
This is a reflection: of love.
Tears streak down, cutting the dry skin.
Yes, I was dry a second ago.
I was dry and cracking,
I pulled myself together by
crying. This is reality: the
night. Being wasted, holding
your breath, so as you don't
accidentally scream. Love.
It's a fickle thing. Run your chipped nails
across your scalp. Wasted
like everything else.
This is romance: one of those nights.
Street light: holy sight.
If the body does really die
one night, and rebirths the next,
the fallen angels save me...

Aging Together

There is a war waging on my skin.
Time pushes it together, collides the ashes of
memories and calls me old.
While you pull them away and stretch
the moments to a timeline of
wonder. You grow me younger,
attached to my skin with your eyes
and words. I will follow the path
you have laid out for me - we
can't tell if we're old or not,
we're too busy doing it together.

Your Eyes Tell Me Things

your eyes tell me things

but you're not the one telling me them
so you won't know what i know
even if you say you do

because i'm talking to your eyes
not you

and they tell me things
little things
big things
cosmic sense of reality
but also the
fragments of probabilities
green things
purple things
white things
clear things
vague things
shit
sentimentality
loss of mentality
awakening of senses
sky things
land things
so many things

because i am talking to your eyes

not you.

Singing My Song

I am singing my song
when I write.
Songs of emptiness
and regret and confused
entailments of life.
So when I sing of the world,
the world is mine
as my melody sweeps the
grass like I am the wind
and the stanzas build a house
like I am the brick.
Therefore, I sing of love,
and you, and the wild nights,
so I may become a part of them
again, so that I may capture
the soft kiss, the passionate hold,
and the soft glow of the waning moon,
so I can house you in my memories,
so I may sing of us, you and me.